# Christmas Song
# of the North

Marsha Bonicatto
Karlyn Holman

**Pfeifer-Hamilton Publishers**
Duluth, Minnesota

*This book is dedicated to my parents
and grandparents, who introduced me
to the wonders of the north woods,
and to my husband, Larry, and our sons,
David, James, and Steven,
who encourage me in all I attempt.*

—Marsha Bonicatto, author

*To Brianna, who has a special way
of communicating and celebrating
with the animal world.*

—Karlyn Holman, illustrator

Pfeifer-Hamilton Publishers
210 West Michigan
Duluth, MN 55802-1908
218-727-0500

*Christmas Song of the North*

Printed by Doosan Dong-A Co., Ltd.
10 9 8 7 6 5 4 3 2 1

Editorial Director: Donald A.Tubesing
Art Director: Joy Morgan Dey

Library of Congress
Catalog Card Number: 97-60279
ISBN 1-57025-145-2
Printed in the Republic of Korea

The north woods are silent, as soft winter snow
Sifts through the bare branches and settles below.
The days are their shortest, the nights long and cold,
Yet spell-binding dramas around us unfold.

All wildlife takes cover in ways that are clever
To keep themselves cozy in spite of the weather.
If we become quiet and listen with care,
We'll soon get acquainted with friends who live there.

Listen now, and sing right along
with this lively north-woods Christmas song.

On the first day
of Christmas,
the north woods
gave to me

**A ruffed grouse
in a pine tree**

*I*n winter, Ruffed Grouse grow feathers on their feet that work just like snowshoes. They often burrow under a protective blanket of snow to keep warm.

On the second day
of Christmas,
the north woods
gave to me

**2** **snowy**
**owls**

and a ruffed grouse
in a pine tree

Most owls hunt for food at night, but Snowy Owls hunt during the day. In spring, they fly north to the Arctic where they nest and raise their families.

On the third day
of Christmas,
the north woods
gave to me

**3 red
squirrels**

**TWO** snowy owls

and a ruffed grouse
in a pine tree

In the fall, these sassy, curious critters gather nuts, seeds, fruit, and mushrooms. Squirrels hide their food in trees and under logs so that later, when the snow falls, they will have plenty to eat.

On the fourth day
of Christmas,
the north woods
gave to me

*4* **sleepy
bears**

**THREE** red squirrels

**TWO** snowy owls

and a ruffed grouse
in a pine tree

*B*lack Bears eat so much in the summer that they get fat. Just before winter, a mother bear and her cubs make a nest of grasses and leaves in a cave or under a fallen tree. Then, they crawl in and sleep all winter.

On the fifth day
of Christmas,
the north woods
gave to me

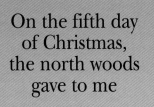

**5 white birch trees**

**FOUR** sleepy bears

**THREE** red squirrels

**TWO** snowy owls

and a ruffed grouse
in a pine tree

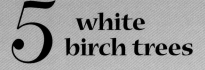

*T*he birch tree's paper-white bark with inky-black lines creates one of nature's many perfect designs. For centuries, Native Americans used this bark to make cooking pots and canoes.

On the sixth day
of Christmas,
the north woods
gave to me

**6** otters
playing

**FIVE** white birch trees

**FOUR** sleepy bears

**THREE** red squirrels

**TWO** snowy owls

and a ruffed grouse
in a pine tree

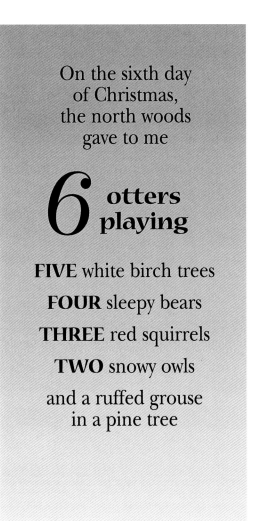

During the winter, otters spend many hours swimming in the cold water hunting for food. But like happy children, they still love to play. For winter fun, they slide down snowbanks on their tummies.

On the seventh day
of Christmas,
the north woods
gave to me

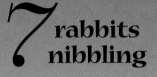

**7 rabbits
nibbling**

**SIX** otters playing

**FIVE** white birch trees

**FOUR** sleepy bears

**THREE** red squirrels

**TWO** snowy owls

and a ruffed grouse
in a pine tree

With their big ears, cottontail rabbits hear very well. With their large back feet they run very fast. Still, they often hide under brush piles during the day and come out at night to eat.

On the eighth day
of Christmas,
the north woods
gave to me

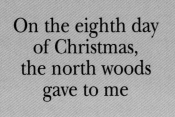 **deer
a-drinking**

**SEVEN** rabbits nibbling

**SIX** otters playing

**FIVE** white birch trees

**FOUR** sleepy bears

**THREE** red squirrels

**TWO** snowy owls

and a ruffed grouse
in a pine tree

When the snow gets deep, White-tailed Deer gather in large groups and stay in one area, resting and eating together during most of the winter. For a special treat, they nibble the tips of cedar trees or dig into the snow for acorns.

On the ninth day
of Christmas,
the north woods
gave to me

**9** **mice
dig-digging**

**EIGHT** deer a-drinking

**SEVEN** rabbits nibbling

**SIX** otters playing

**FIVE** white birch trees

**FOUR** sleepy bears

**THREE** red squirrels

**TWO** snowy owls

and a ruffed grouse
in a pine tree

*D*eer Mice snuggle together in warm underground nests where they have stored seeds to eat. At night, these small creatures pop out of their nests and run across the snow, leaving tiny tracks that you can see the next morning.

On the tenth day
of Christmas,
the north woods
gave to me

# 10 fish a-swimming

**NINE** mice dig-digging

**EIGHT** deer a-drinking

**SEVEN** rabbits nibbling

**SIX** otters playing

**FIVE** white birch trees

**FOUR** sleepy bears

**THREE** red squirrels

**TWO** snowy owls

and a ruffed grouse
in a pine
tree

In the lakes and streams of the north woods, fish stay comfortable all winter long. When the ice forms a roof over their heads, they don't feel the cold. They swim after minnows and water bugs whenever they're hungry.

On the eleventh day
of Christmas,
the north woods
gave to me

*11* **chickadees
calling**

**TEN** fish a-swimming

**NINE** mice dig-digging

**EIGHT** deer a-drinking

**SEVEN** rabbits nibbling

**SIX** otters playing

**FIVE** white birch trees

**FOUR** sleepy bears

**THREE** red squirrels

**TWO** snowy owls

and a ruffed grouse
in a pine tree

Chickadees appear very formal
in their black and white feathers,
fluffed up to keep out the cold.
But they are really one of the north
wood's friendliest birds. They call
to each other by singing their
own name.

On the twelfth day
of Christmas,
the north woods
gave to me

# 12 wolves a-howling

**ELEVEN** chickadees calling

**TEN** fish a-swimming

**NINE** mice dig-digging

**EIGHT** deer a-drinking

**SEVEN** rabbits nibbling

**SIX** otters playing

**FIVE** white birch trees

**FOUR** sleepy bears

**THREE** red squirrels

**TWO** snowy owls

and a ruffed grouse
in a pine tree

Wolves live in a family group called a pack. They all cooperate by hunting together, sharing their food, and caring for the young pups. Sometimes their mournful howls can be heard on winter nights as they talk to each other.

*Shhhhh . . .*

All is now quiet.
The north woods are sleeping,
Under a blanket of snow.

## Author
## Marsha Bonicatto

Marsha Walstrom Bonicatto was born in northern Minnesota but has lived most of her adult life in the Upper Peninsula of Michigan. In their north woods surroundings, she and her husband, Larry, have raised their three sons with a keen appreciation for the wonders of nature. This is Marsha's first book.

---

## Illustrator
## Karlyn Holman

Karlyn Holman's watercolors reflect a special exuberance for the Lake Superior region. She is a full-time artist and has operated her own studio-gallery since 1968. Karlyn teaches high-spirited watercolor workshops throughout the U.S. and on location around the world. She lives in Washburn, Wisconsin, with her husband, Gary. This is Karlyn's fourth book.